Longshore Drift

Longshore Drift

A radio-poem

Katrina Porteous

Linocuts by James Dodds

Jardine Press Ltd
2011

For the
Inshore Fishermen of the East Coast

Jardine Press Ltd 2011
1st edition (hardback):
Jardine Press Ltd 2005
Text © Katrina Porteous
Linocuts © James Dodds
Book design by Catherine Clark
Printed by Healeys, Ipswich

ISBN 978 0 9565495 1 8

www.jardinepress.co.uk
www.katrinaporteous.co.uk
www.jamesdodds.co.uk

Cover: 'Stern of an Aldeburgh Beach Boat', © James Dodds, 2004, Oil on linen

Introduction

When I visited Aldeburgh as writer-in-residence to its Poetry Festival in October and November 2002, the Suffolk coast was new to me. Its physical geography surprised me, its stony shores unexpectedly bleaker and more exposed than the sandy beaches of Northumberland. In the four weeks I spent there, however, I soon found many similarities to home – particularly in the crisis facing the longshore fishermen. Dwindling fish-stocks, low prices due to imported and farmed fish, and crippling quotas and regulations designed to prevent over-fishing by much larger boats, meant that the longshoremen were finding it increasingly difficult to make a living. When I wrote this poem, seven boats fished from the beach at Aldeburgh. Two years later, only three were left. That number remains about the same in 2011.

The Suffolk longshoremen fish according to season: that November, they were using long lines to catch cod, trammel nets for soles and sea bass, pots for crabs, and drift nets for herring. As in Northumberland, the longshoremen's small-scale, traditional methods are generally more sustainable than those of bigger boats. Whether they fish from clinker-built wooden boats or modern fibreglass vessels, their fishing days and the weight of gear that they carry are restricted by the boat's length, usually between twenty and twenty-six feet. Even with modern navigational aids, the men are extremely reliant upon traditional knowledge. They work with the sea, not against it, and their lives depend upon their respect for it.

Although it was late in the year, I was extremely fortunate to go fishing off Sizewell and Aldeburgh. I was fascinated to see long lining and drift netting at close quarters. Once staples of fishing in Northumberland, these methods have long since vanished from the North East coast, where small boat fishermen now largely rely upon crabs and lobsters. Small-scale drift netting and long lining are much less damaging to fish-stocks than trawling and seine-netting: fish trapped in a trawl, if under-size or over-quota, are thrown back dead; but those hooked on a long line are still alive. This made me all the more aware of the value of the longshoremen's skills and knowledge. As I crunched along the Suffolk beaches, I reflected on the mutability of that coast. I looked out towards the lost city of Dunwich, once one of England's biggest ports, now almost entirely sunk beneath the sea. I thought of the decline of the longshoremen's way of life, handed down for generations, and now vanishing before our eyes. I have tried in this poem to capture a glimpse of what we are losing.

Longshore Drift was written for radio, and much of it is based upon interviews which I recorded with the fishermen. The broadcast version was punctuated by snatches of real speech. In the text, the reader will hear echoes of the men's voices, describing their methods: at one time, when catches were plentiful, twenty-four, or even twelve or fourteen long lines, known as 'a dozen an' two', was the self-imposed limit for every small boat on the Suffolk coast. The men speak of their particular skills: how, before electronic and satellite equipment became available, they navigated using compass, lead-line and landmark – 'Fourteen fathom and a wet wrist', 'House in the Clouds on the white flats' – so locating fishing grounds like Kettle Bottom and Lord Louis', and wrecks such as the Magdapur and the Inner and Outer Sweepers. These names, the local dialect names for the sea-bed flora and fauna, and a few of the superstitions of the coast ('I hung out the washing as we left on the Monday…') appear in the poem as chants and charms. Other dialect words are explained in the glossary.

A radio-poem allows a writer to extend the musical possibilities of poetry. In this edition, these possibilities are given a further visual interpretation. Longshore Drift is composed of two 'voices', which are indicated by plain and italic text. The poem is arranged on facing pages. To begin with, each voice speaks separately; but, as the poem continues, the two voices often speak or chant simultaneously. Where this happens, text appears on both left and right-hand pages, plain and italic voices aligned alongside each other. At other times, the two voices speak antiphonally. This is indicated by plain and italic variation within a line. The two voices are not static; they shift in relation to each other from one side of the audio spectrum to the other and between left and right-hand page. The broadcast version of 'Longshore Drift' included sea, engine and radio-sounds which I recorded on the beaches, in the boats, and in the fishermen's sheds. These sounds are incorporated into the musical texture of the poem, and are indicated in the text in bold.

I am delighted that this poem should appear alongside the work of James Dodds, an artist whose work I admire enormously, and who truly understands the sea and those who live with it. I should like to thank him, his wife Catherine who designed this book, and all the people who helped in the research, writing and production of this poem; in particular the late Annie Healey, Michael and Kay Laskey, Penny Berry, and the fishermen of Aldeburgh, Sizewell and Dunwich, especially 'Dodger' Holmes, Rodney Burns, Dean Fryer and Noel Cattermole. To Dean and Noel, special thanks for putting up with my endless questions and for taking me to sea.

Longshore Drift was commissioned by BBC Radio 3 and first broadcast on 'The Verb' on February 15th 2003, produced by Julian May.

Katrina Porteous, 2011

'There's only one boss when you're off there, and that's the sea.
And if you don't respect it, God help you!'

Rodney Burns,
Aldeburgh fisherman.

Longshore Drift

Crash of sea on shingle:

In the dark, the fizz of the sea on the shore
Is the hiss of burning, of the single star
That hangs in the lamp-glow, low on the horizon,
Till the slow wheel tilts and the sky lightens
Over shingle and marshes, bent-hills and heather;

And the longshoreman shoulders his boat down the ladder
Of skids on the flints like a horse by the bridle;

And the winch jerks.
The wheel spins
And the warp tightens.

Sudden loud chug of winch:

Dog whelk,
Anemone,
Barnacle
And shipworm;
Sea-cabbage,
Spotty dog,
Brittle star
And keelworm;
Peelers,
Razors,
Weevers,
Stingers,
Featherweed,
Coralweed,
Deadmen's fingers.

Two voices chant simultaneously:

Dog whelk, anemone, barnacle and shipworm,
Sea-cabbage, spotty dog, brittle star and keelworm;
Peelers, razors, weevers, stingers,
Featherweed, coralweed, deadmen's fingers.

I hung out the washing as we left on the Monday,
Headed for the sea in a pea-green jersey.
A pig in the back yard squealed like a baby.
The sky burned red and the moon looked hazy.

Dog whelk,
Anemone,
Barnacle
And shipworm;
Sea-cabbage,
Spotty dog,
Brittle star
And keelworm;
Peelers,
Razors,
Weevers,
Stingers,
Featherweed,
Coralweed,
Deadmen's fingers.

Dog whelk, anemone, barnacle and shipworm,
Sea-cabbage, spotty dog, brittle star and keelworm;
Peelers, razors, weevers, stingers,
Featherweed, coralweed, deadmen's fingers.

Down Crag Path I bowed to the clergy,
Nodded to a nun and a woman in a doorway.
Gonna shoot my last new fleet on a Friday,
Whistle on the deck till the wind turns dodgy.

Winch ends abruptly.

Crunch of footsteps, sea on shingle;
antiphonal voices:

Show me a road to the sea. *Reeds, rushes.*
Weaving through marshes. *Not to be trusted.*
Salt sea channels. Runnels. *A river.*
Treacherous. Dangerous. *Claw-marks: water.*

Sky like an ink-stain. *Rain tonight.*
An egret, rising. *Silent flight*
Over the water that holds the light;

The sodden light, neither land nor sea,
Immense, absorbent. *Rushes, reeds,*
Stretching away to the vanished harbour.

A forest of masts. *A city of ships.*
Close the mouth. *Seal the lips.*
Let the years and the water do their work.
Treacherous. Dangerous. *Not to be trusted.*

Sea and blustery wind:

Out there, the sea: a sheet
Of tin-foil, shaken out,

A boiling, pewter-grey,
Copper-tinged alloy;

A growl, a snarl, a frown.
It darkens like a stain,

White-veined, white-fretted, brown
And snagged with angry light;

It glitters in the bright
Spilt metal of the sun.

Fade down wind gradually:

The small boats face the waves,
Their broad, white clinker curves

A cockle's rippled shell –
Something the sea has made.

The brent geese gather and go,
And the herring, on their journey,

And the longshoremen in their sheds
Watch the weather, and wait.

End sea.

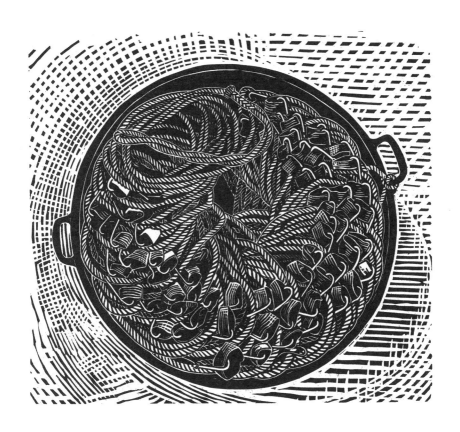

Voice inside:

Old Dodger's telling tales
In the Bug's Nest. Down the road,

Tootsie's rehooking like a lunatic
And Noel baits his bath of lines.

They have seen them flower and vanish,
The grey-green rags of sea-kale,

The poppies, clawing the pebbles –
The great port of Dunwich.

And the wind blows over the bent-hills;
And the last big boat leaves Lowestoft;

And the tide's edge frets at the shingle.
How quickly the weather changes.

Radio in shed – a navigation warning.
Cheerful music punctuated by stormy weather report
and static disturbance:

Ten a.m. Dean's shed is full
Of strip-light, music and the smell
Of crab-meat, winkled from its shell.

At a bench the two men stand,
Each with a teaspoon in his hand,
Dean to the claws, Paul to the backs.

Michael's balanced on a box,
Arranging small, square, snowy blocks
Of frozen squid on rows of hooks
That barely touch: a lifetime's skill.

Passing customers who call
For newspaper parcels of cod and sole

Pause at the door, stare inside,
Consume the three men with their eyes –

Salt-steeped, weary from the sea
In boots and oilskins, they appear
More present, anchored, and alive.

A static hiss. The music stops.
Dean picks a sole out of the box,
Peels its skin off like a glove.

Gale force eight, the radio warns.
He shrugs. Four lines still to haul.

It's more than fish his callers buy.

Static crackle from radio – volume increases:
Coastguard announcing south-westerly gales.

Winch – sudden, loud:

We've always lived on the edge, boy;
Small boats, lines and nets.
We've always fished as the old men fished,
And the old men showed the sea respect;

For they'd wait for the fish in their season,
Shootin' a dozen an' two.
I'll tell you, there's just one skipper out there
And that's not you.

Winch splutters and cranks down.

When a dozen an' two was your limit
Your twelve long lines might fetch
A hundred stone. Now a hundred lines
Won't land you ten. And there's the catch.

Technology's killed the fishing.
Sea never gets no rest.
Now politics' gonna finish the job
With the law like a millstone round our necks;

And it's duck, dodge, bend like a reed;
Small boats, little gear.
If we was to land every fish we caught
They'd still be there another year.

Kettle Bottom, Lord Louis', Sugar Boat and Shipwash;
Nape's Bank, the Onion, In and Out the Dingle.
Inner Bank, Eva Wit, Magdapur, the Ridge;
Inner Sweeper, Outer Sweeper, In and Out the Dingle.

Kettle Bottom, Lord Louis', Sugar Boat and Shipwash;
Nape's Bank, the Onion, In and Out the Dingle.
Inner Bank, Eva Wit, Magdapur, the Ridge;
Inner Sweeper, Outer Sweeper, In and Out the Dingle.

Kettle Bottom, Lord Louis', Sugar Boat and Shipwash;
Nape's Bank, the Onion, In and Out the Dingle.
Inner Bank, Eva Wit, Magdapur, the Ridge;
Inner Sweeper, Outer Sweeper, In and Out the Dingle.

Sea – fade down:

Kettle Bottom,
Lord Louis',
Sugar Boat
And Shipwash;
Nape's Bank,
The Onion,
In and Out the Dingle.

Inner Bank,
Eva Wit,
Magdapur,
The Ridge;
Inner Sweeper,
Outer Sweeper,
In and Out the Dingle.

Hand over fist over
Fist over hand,
Quick as a sprinter,
Haul the long line.

Salt spray
And the free hooks spinning,
Jerk of the wrist
And a big cod writhing.

Kettle Bottom, Lord Louis',
Sugar Boat and Shipwash;
Nape's Bank, the Onion,
In and Out the Dingle.

Inner Bank, Eva Wit,
Magdapur, the Ridge;
Inner Sweeper, Outer Sweeper,
In and Out the Dingle.

Fade up boat's radio –
electronic beat of music, static, weather:

Stop. Fast.
Haul hard.
Fist over hand over
Hand over fist – And it's

Snoods, spray
And the free hooks flying,
Flick of the wrist
And a cod thumps down.

End radio.

Kettle Bottom, Lord Louis',
Sugar Boat and Shipwash;
Nape's Bank, the Onion,
In and Out the Dingle.

Inner Bank, Eva Wit,
Magdapur, the Ridge;
Inner Sweeper, Outer Sweeper,
In and Out the Dingle

Fourteen fathom and a wet wrist,
Nothing but the lead and a watch and compass
Southwold down to Orford Ness.
Better than magic, GPS.
Gap in the hedge. Chimneys in one.
Tree on the white house. End of the harbour
Clear of the green church roof. Remember,
House in the Clouds on the white flats
Finds you the Mag in the deeper water.
If the jails come on you've got the Inner Sweeper.
House in the Clouds and the water tower.
Church on the jail. Yes, I remember
Pitch black. Thick fog.
Fourteen fathom and a wet wrist.
Nothing but the lead and a watch and compass
Southwold down to Orford Ness.

Hand over fist over
Fist over hand,
Quick as a sprinter,
Haul the long line.

Salt spray
And the free hooks spinning,
Jerk of the wrist
And a big cod writhing.

Grab the buff
And haul the blue tow
Tight in the water.
Heave the big anchor.

Hand over fist,
Fist over hand,
Quick as a sprinter,
Haul the long line.

Fade up boat's radio:

Steer the boat carefully,
Inch her ahead,
Tracing the uneven
Line on the sea-floor.

Fist over hand over
Hand over fist,
And a long tug at nothing
As the line comes fast; and it's

Salt spray
And the free hooks spinning,
Jerk of the wrist
And a big cod writhing.

Stop. Fast.
Haul hard.
Fist over hand over
Hand over fist – And it's

My body's at ease on the water,

More than on the land.

I'm at home on the sea. I was born for this life.

I call myself a happy man:

Though I've slogged out me guts for nothin'

But heartache an' little pay,

And I wouldn't want to see me own boy battered

As the sea has battered me many a day.

For how can you call it a livin',

Winter with no cod,

And the boats gettin' fewer on the beach each year?

I'm the last of the line. You can call me mad,

Music from boat's radio begins – electronic beat:

Snoods, spray
And the free hooks flying,
Flick of the wrist
And a cod thumps down.

Then a break in the rhythm
For the first small anchor:
Loose coyp.
Let her away! And it's

Fist over hand over
Hand over fist,
And a long tug at nothing
As the line comes fast; and it's

Steer the boat carefully
This way, that way,
Nosing ahead
And a dead stop. Nothing.

Stop. And steady and
Steady, then – Stop.
And a yank of the snood
As a cod flies off,

But it's out on the boundless water

Under the endless sky,

I think of the people I meet on the land

And I know there's envy in their eyes.

For how can you call it a livin',

Bound to an office desk?

When you see that sun come up – God knows,

It's a hard haul an' little rest

When you're haulin' for home, me darlin',

When you're givin' it all you can –

*And salt spray
And the free hooks spinning,
Jag of the prawl
And a big cod flapping,*

*Fist over hand over
Hand over fist,
And it's coil and stop,
And steady, and – patience!*

**Whistle, and Coastguard, louder:
'Approaches to Boston, Freeman Channel…'**

Sudden crash of sea, then fade down:

Miles of loose stones
Banked like ballast;
Looks like JCBs
Have crunched it,
Clawed it, raked it,
Pulverised it;

Till it stands
A spoil-heap-high
Embankment,
Muffling the sea,
Its lee-side quiet
Colonised

But if I was to die in my sleep tonight

I'd die
        a happy
                man.

By stonecrop, dock
And dry white hooks
Of poppy-heads;
Their anchor-flukes
Scrape and scrabble
On the ledge.

This narrow ridge –
Steep, headlong slide
And pebble-rattle,
Shingle-crunch,
Rasp and gravel-grind –
This edge

Is all that's holding
Back the tide.

Loud sea:

Dog whelk,
Anemone,
Barnacle
And shipworm;
Sea-cabbage,
Spotty dog,
Brittle star
And keelworm;
Peelers,
Razors,
Weevers,
Stingers,
Featherweed,
Coralweed,
Deadmen's fingers.

Dog whelk, anemone, barnacle and shipworm,
Sea-cabbage, spotty dog, brittle star and keelworm;
Peelers, razors, weevers, stingers,
Featherweed, coralweed, deadmen's fingers.

Good luck, bad luck; follow all the tideways
Over the cold sea's starry highway;
Stone with a hole and a little piece of coal
In the bottom of your pocket and we'll sail home safely.

Surge of sea on shingle – fade down:

This is a coast of stones.
A chest of bones.

Quartz and chert, a mass
Harder than glass,

Carried from elsewhere, no
Intention of staying put.

No intention at all.
Contingent. Accidental.

Never meant to last.
Nothing here holds fast.

Footsteps on shingle. Fade up sea:

Show me a road to the sea.
You'd nearly think it was meant

To stand, a monument
To permanence, the shore.

This is the tale we are told.
This is the lie in the bones.

This is the line you must cross.
This is the coast of stones.

Sea surge, loud.

Glossary

Buff – buoy

Coyp – rope attaching small anchor to end of long line

Deadmen's fingers – a type of sea anemone

Dozen an' two – fourteen long lines, once a self-imposed limit amongst longshoremen

GPS – global positioning satellite navigation system

Spotty dog – dog-fish

Stingers – sting-ray

Peelers – soft green crabs

Prawl – gaff

Snoods – lengths of twine attaching hooks to long lines

Tow – rope

Weever – a stinging fish

Katrina Porteous was born in Aberdeen and now lives on the Northumberland coast. She has written many poems for radio, including 'Dunstanburgh' (Smokestack Books 2004), 'The Refuge Box' and 'An Ill Wind'. Her illustrated history of Northumbrian fishing, 'The Bonny Fisher Lad', appeared in 2003, and her poems about Northumbrian fishing traditions are published in 'The Lost Music' (Bloodaxe 1996), 'The Wund an' the Wetter' (Iron Press 1999) and 'The Blue Lonnen' (Jardine Press 2007).

James Dodds is an artist and former shipwright whose paintings and prints have been touring the British Isles since 2001 as an exhibition called 'Shipshape'. His first book was an illustrated edition of George Crabbe's 'Peter Grimes'. In 'Longshore Drift', James returns to Aldeburgh beach 20 years later. It was fellow-artist and linocutter Penny Berry who first encouraged James to send a copy of his book with poet Martin Newell, 'Song of the Waterlily', to Katrina. From this initial contact grew the wish to collaborate.

Other Books from Jardine Press Ltd

Peter Grimes
by George Crabbe. Linocuts by James Dodds.
Jardine Press 1984, 1987, 2000. 210 x 150mm, 32pp.
ISBN 0 9509270 0 7. Paperback.

Wild Man of Orford
by Allan Drummond. Woodcuts by James Dodds.
Jardine Press 1995, 2002. 180 x 180mm, 36pp.
ISBN 0 9525594 0 4. Paperback.

Black Shuck
by Martin Newell. Linocuts by James Dodds.
Jardine Press 1999. 220 x 150mm, 24pp.
ISBN 0 9525594 8 X. Paperback.

Alphabet of Boats
Text and linocuts by James Dodds.
Jardine Press 1998. 115 x 115mm,32pp.
ISBN 0 9525594 6 3. Hardback.

ABC of Boat Bits
Text and linocuts by James Dodds.
Jardine Press 2000. 115 x 150mm, 36pp.
ISBN 0 9539472 0 3. Hardback.

The Song of the Waterlily
by Martin Newell. Linocuts by James Dodds
Jardine Press Ltd October 2003. 200mm x 200mm, 52pp.
ISBN 0 9539472 4. Hardback.

The Blue Lonnen
by Katrina Porteous. Photographs by Nigel Shuttleworth, paintings by James Dodds
Jardine Press Ltd October 2007. 140mm x 210mm, 48pp.
ISBN 978-0-9552035-5-8. Hardback